A. W. Sherwood.
Aug. 1949.

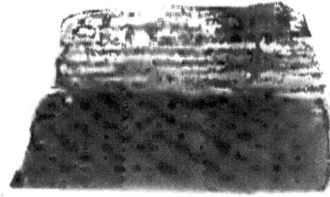

A LADY OF THE MINOAN COURT

From *The Annual of the British School at Athens*

[*Frontispiece*

The Minoans

by George Glasgow

Jonathan Cape
Eleven Gower Street, London

First published March, 1923
Second impression April, 1923

Printed in Great Britain by Butler & Tanner, Frome and London

THIS BOOK IS DEDICATED
TO
RONALD MONTAGU BURROWS
MY GREAT FRIEND AND TEACHER

PREFACE

SIR ARTHUR EVANS' renewed campaign of excavation in Crete has again attracted considerable public attention to the remarkable disclosures of the last twenty years. Sir Arthur Evans himself is at present engaged in compiling in three big volumes the consecutive story of Minoan civilization as revealed by his own excavations. The present writer is convinced that the story of Cretan discovery is such as to appeal to the imagination of a wide public who have no specialist interest in archæology. The story has all the interest of adventure and exploration. This book is an attempt to meet what such a public wants. I have tried to give a general picture of the world which existed in the Mediterranean four thousand years ago, and of the amazing process by which it has been revealed, so that it can be understood by those totally unacquainted with classical study, and I have tried to give it in one hour's reading. For those who want to go further I give references to other books. It must be understood that this

7

Preface

book does not aim at an exact account of the archæological position as it exists to-day. With new excavations being carried out this very year, and with new material in the hands of the excavators, as yet unpublished and un-digested, any attempt to be strictly up to date would merely mean the progressive and inde-finite postponement of the book. The broad lines of the discovery of Minoan civilization are clear, and in the writer's opinion, even because a new campaign of excavation is now started, ought to be presented now in a form to be easily understood. The results of the dis-coveries of this spring, for instance, add im-portant details to our knowledge—some of which I have incorporated—but do not affect fundamentals.

Some of the substance of the fol-lowing chapters was published in 1920 and 1921 in *Discovery*, to the Editor of which I am grateful for permission to re-publish them. In a somewhat different form the substance was also published by me in 1914–1915 in the *National Home Reading Magazine*.

It is to my friend Dr. Ronald Montagu Burrows that I, in common with thousands, owe my interest in Crete. He died on May 14, 1920, before his time. He was incredibly,

Preface

challengingly young and vigorous both in
appearance and in activity, and at fifty-two
was producing work at the top of his brilliant
form. His work was a mixture of youth and
maturity such as one does not often find. In
1907, when he first published his *Discoveries
in Crete*, men were confused by the avalanche
of discovery in Crete which had been going
on since the opening of the century. Burrows's achievement—for which scholars and
the intellectual public have ever since been
grateful—was to give a comprehensive and
interpretive account of the whole revelation
and to place it in its perspective. Before that
even scholars as a whole had not seen wood
for trees.

Dr. Burrows's own excavations at Pylos and
Sphacteria and at Rhitsona were typical of him.
He cleared up the narrative and established
the good faith of the historian Thucydides.
Scholars had in vain tried to find any trace of
the fortifications said by Thucydides to have
been erected there by the Spartans in the
Peloponnesian war. Only a few months before
Burrows first went out—he was then a young
man who did not know the difficulty of what
he attempted—a celebrated geographer, Dr.
Grundy, had explored the site and reported
that there was no trace of the fortifications.

Preface

Burrows discovered substantial remains hidden away under the brushwood, and succeeded in proving that they fully corresponded with Thucydides's account.

I am grateful to Professor R. S. Conway and to Sir Arthur Evans for reading my manuscript and helping me with suggestions; but neither must be held responsible for anything that appears in the book.

1922.

CONTENTS

LIST OF ILLUSTRATIONS

Chapter 1 : *Crete the Forerunner of Greece*

M R. VENISELOS was brought up in Crete. It is not the first time in history that Crete has passed on her products to Greece and to Europe. Four thousand years ago the very foundations of Greek and of European civilization were laid in Crete, which was then mistress of the sea and the dominant factor in the Ægean. Yet we none of us were aware of this until Sir Arthur Evans, a few years ago, began digging in Crete. When Mr. Veniselos was a boy the very existence of a prehistoric Cretan civilization was unknown. Our knowledge of it has been almost entirely revealed since 1900. In this short time the spades of Sir Arthur Evans have revolutionized our whole conception of the early history of Europe. Excavation at Knossos, Phæstos and other sites in Crete has disclosed the existence of a people whose form of civilization, the earliest in Europe, flourished long before recorded history begins. It has told us about their daily life, games, amusements, art, religion,

13

The Minoans

writing (though the language is not yet understood) ; their physical type, dress, the homes they lived in. The fashion of the women's dresses, as revealed on ornaments and other art relics, with an open neck and flounced skirts, made a French scholar exclaim : " Mais ce sont des Parisiennes ! "

A big palace, as big as Buckingham Palace, has been unearthed at Knossos. It has a drainage system which an eminent Italian archæologist, Dr. Halbherr, has described as " absolutely English," and which certainly forestalls the hydraulic engineering of the nineteenth century. This four thousand years ago.

The digging in Crete has created all the excitement of exploration. When the painted panel was discovered giving a sensational bull-baiting scene from a Minoan circus-show, or the Phæstos disc covered with picture writing, or the fresco painting of the Cupbearer at Knossos, the excitement reached its height. It was not confined to the excavators. An old workman who was on night duty watching the Cupbearer fresco during the delicate operation of its removal, was woke up by disturbing dreams and declared after that " The whole place was full of ghosts."

Charles Kingsley has no doubt turned in

his grave. When he wrote *The Heroes* he was writing, as he himself explained, a fairy story for his children. He little knew that his fairy story was in many ways historical truth. He wrote, for instance, that the palace of King Minos at Knossos was like a marble hill. He did not know that there actually lived a King Minos in Crete, and that his palace, standing on a hill at Knossos, was built, if not of marble, at any rate of stone.

Up to the last half-century the whole story of classical Greece, as taught in the schools and in the Universities, was regarded as something original, as the beginning of things springing suddenly, like the mythical Athene, into life. The sculpture, architecture, philosophy, oratory, and drama of the fifth century B.C., were accepted unquestioningly and with awe as the spontaneous first-fruits of Greek genius. The history of Greece, as then understood, went back only to the eighth century B.C., beyond which were the Dark Ages and nothing. Before the time of Æschylus, Sophocles, and Euripides it is true there had been a problematic poet, half mythical, half real, elusive and shadowy, known as Homer. The fact that he was represented as having been born in nine separate places was an illustration of the vagueness in which the poet's identity was enveloped. He (or they, if his poems were a composite work) had sung of deeds and of men who seemed to echo from those Dark Ages. Whatever speculation there was as to Homer himself and his identity, no one ever doubted that if he was a real person he certainly was the first real person that European history could establish. During the last twenty years he has been shown to have been not the beginning but the end of an enormous phase of Greek and European history.

Now that the real beginnings of Greek civilization are beginning to be known, it strikes one as remarkable that up to now they should have been so completely buried in two senses. It is the more remarkable because a good deal was known about other corresponding origins in the Near East. In Egypt and Babylonia the old traditions had been passed on by later generations to Greek writers, who preserved, imperfectly it is true, the necessary connecting links. In the case of Greek civilization not only were there no stepping-stones back to the corresponding phase ; it did not even seem to occur to anybody that there had been such a phase. The unquestioning and complacent acceptance as myths (which is the same thing as the tacit and complete disbelief) of the epic stories which centred round Agamemnon and the Homeric heroes was never challenged up to the middle of the last century. The historian Grote, for instance, declared that " to analyse the fables and to elicit from them any trustworthy particular facts " would be " a fruitless attempt " (*History of Greece*, 2nd edition, 1849, p. 223).

Such was the outlook of Grote's contemporaries. Then an important thing happened. A poor boy named Schliemann had been told these Greek fables by his father, and to his child's mind the stories appeared as literally true. One day a drunken miller came into the grocer's shop where he worked, and began to recite some lines of Homer. Schliemann was fascinated, and, so the story goes, spent all his spare cash in whisky wherewith to encourage the miller to repeat the lines again and again ; and then prayed God that he might some day have the happiness of learning Greek himself. His literal faith in the "myths" remained with him, and he made up his mind to find the walls of Troy. Being poor he had to spend a lifetime of hard saving before he was in a position to put his faith to the test. Late in life, however, he had saved enough money for the purpose and went to Hissarlik, the spot in Asia Minor where the town of Troy was said to have stood. He began digging

B

The Minoans

into the earth, and to his joy discovered the buried walls of a town. It was proved later that the walls he discovered belonged not to the Homeric city, as Schliemann naturally assumed, but to another city which had existed on the same site a thousand years earlier. He had dug within and through the circle of the Homeric walls without discovering them. From Troy he went to Mycenæ and Tiryns on the Greek mainland, and there discovered the visible relics of the Homeric stories centering on the Greek mainland. Schliemann's achievement was to establish the historical existence of the "Mycenæan civilization." We now know that this civilization flourished from about 1400 B.C. to 1100 B.C. It is a romantic story of the way in which Schliemann justified his simple faith in the historic background of the Homeric poems. Schliemann deserved the explorer's satisfaction which he enjoyed, and which manifested itself on one occasion when he sent a telegram to the King of the Hellenes announcing that he had found the tomb of Agamemnon at Mycenæ. One wishes that it had been literally true, as Schliemann thought it was. In any case it was he who laid the foundations for the whole structure of modern prehistoric research in the Eastern Mediterranean.

Crete the Forerunner of Greece

The most exciting and the most important part of that research has been the opening up of Crete. The Cretan discoveries of Sir Arthur Evans and other excavators, British, American and Italian, have proved that the Mycenæan culture revealed by Schliemann was itself a late and even decadent phase of a great Mediterranean civilization which had its centre in Crete.

Chapter 2 : *The Sea-Faring People of Crete*

THE primitive Ægean people played a great part in the activities of the Near East. They existed for several thousand years, and there are traces of their activity on every shore of the Eastern Mediterranean. Crete, as Homer says, was the land " in the midst of the wine-dark ocean, fair and rich, with the waters all around " (" Odyssey," xix. 172). It was the natural centre towards which the mainlands of Greece, Asia Minor, and Egypt converged, especially as its irregular coast afforded good harbours for the small ships of that time.

The first settlement of man in Crete took place at Knossos, in the later or " Neolithic " Stone Age. This fact is established by the nature of the relics found at the lowest level in the excavations, the level which represents the earliest period in time. Phæstos, on the south side of the island, received its first inhabitants at a later date, as is made clear by the pottery that has been discovered there.

The Sea-Faring People of Crete

This is a typical instance of the value of pottery as archæological evidence. The earliest ware found at Knossos is unornamented ; the next is improved by " incised lines "—that is, lines cut in the clay with a pointed instrument and often filled in, for greater effect, with a white substance. At Phæstos, on the other hand, the pottery found lowest down is already in this second stage in its artistic evolution, the inference being that the men who settled there took the art with them at the point to which it had been developed by the Knossians.

After the " Stone " Age came the " Bronze " Age. Men realized that not stone, but a mixture of copper and tin, provided the best material for instruments. A picturesque touch is added to this discovery by an Italian archæologist, Angelo Mosso, who in *The Dawn of Civilization* gives reason for believing that, even at so remote a period, the tin was brought to Crete from Cornwall. He goes so far as to point out the actual caravan route by which the tin was transported. It was during this Bronze Age, which lasted about 2,000 years, that Cretan civilization reached its highest level. Sir Arthur Evans has given to it the picturesque name " Minoan," and has divided it into three stages—Early, Middle,

The Minoans

Late—each with three subdivisions. Early Minoan I (E.M.I) begins about 2800 B.C., Late Minoan III (L.M. III) ends about 1100 B.C. (See *The Discoveries in Crete*, by Dr. Ronald M. Burrows, p. 98.) These nine periods are a happy play upon " the nine seasons " during which Homer speaks of King Minos as reigning in Knossos : " And in Crete is Knossos, a great city, and in it Minos ruled for nine seasons, the bosom friend of mighty Zeus." ("Odyssey," xix. 179). The term " Minoan " should be carefully distinguished from " Mycenæan." After Schliemann's discoveries at Mycenæ and Tiryns, the term " Mycenæan" was used in a general sense, to cover the whole prehistoric Ægean civilization ; but now that Crete has put Mycenæ into its right perspective, the term " Minoan " is used to indicate the earlier and greater phase, while " Mycenæan " merely covers the latest phase ; the whole being designated " Ægean." There is, to complete the nomenclature, a further epithet, " Cycladic," which is sometimes substituted for " Minoan " when one speaks exclusively of the island sites outside of Crete.

With the fall of Knossos, which took place shortly before 1400 B.C.—I adopt Dr. Burrows's dating—the centre of influence in

The Sea-Faring People of Crete

the Ægean passed over from Crete to the mainland of Greece, and the true " Mycenæan " period started. Thereafter followed the Dark Ages, which themselves immediately preceded " historical " Greece. Recorded Greek history begins about 800 B.C.

Chapter 3 ; *Minos and the Mino-taur*

IF the nine Minoan periods into which Sir Arthur Evans has divided the Bronze Age in Crete are primarily a fanciful play upon the " nine seasons " of King Minos's reign in Knossos, the system of dating itself is by no means fanciful. It rests on a solid basis. It has been made possible mainly by the fact that the ancient Cretans were sea-farers. Cretan products were exported to Egypt, and have been found there alongside Egyptian deposits of more or less known date. Hence a system of sequence-dating can be established. It is obvious that a Cretan vase found side by side with an Egyptian vase of 2500 B.C. belongs to an earlier period than one found with deposits of 1500 B.C. This fixing of land-marks is the first step. The second is to assign to them absolute dates in the terms of our own chronology. Owing to the fact that Egyptian dates (within at least certain limits) are known in terms of our own, and that Egyptian ware has been found in Crete as well as Cretan in Egypt, equation is possible. The chief difficulty is that Egyptian chronology is itself variously interpreted, and one particular version has had to be fixed on for comparison. Three convenient and easily-remembered landmarks have been established :

(*a*) Early Minoan II corresponds to Dynasty VI in the early Dynastic Period of Egypt, circa 2500 B.C. As the evidence for this equation is slight compared with that for the other two, it must be accepted with reserve at present as a good working hypothesis.

(*b*) Middle Minoan II corresponds to Dynasties XII and XIII in the Middle Kingdom of Egypt, circa 1900-1700 B.C.

(*c*) Late Minoan II corresponds to Dynasty XVIII in the New Empire of Egypt, circa 1500 B.C.

It is pottery again that has been the basis of this chronological reconstruction. The beautiful Cretan many-coloured ware of the Middle Minoan period, exported to Egypt during the Middle Kingdom and found with objects of the Twelfth Dynasty, forms the chief equating factor between those two periods, and the other equations are based on similar facts. Pottery can be made in some cases to fix approximate dates without the help of equations. Buildings, for instance, cannot

have stood later than the date of the particular
kind of pottery found in their ruins.   It may
be remarked in passing that the Egyptian
trade thus indicated by the remains of Cretan
pottery was responsible for a great improvement in that pottery.   Towards the end of
the early Minoan period the two great inven-
tions of the firing furnace and the potter's
wheel were brought to Crete from Egypt.
Before that time the vases had been roughly
shaped by hand and hardened in the sun.   They
now were " thrown " with such a mastery of
technique as to attain egg-shell thinness.

Traces of commercial intercourse overseas
can be found as far back as the Neolithic Age.
Among the deposits of stone implements in
Crete are great quantities of obsidian knives,
and the only source of obsidian in the Ægean
was the island of Melos.   Obsidian is a kind
of volcanic glass which flakes off into layers,
giving a natural edge.   Excavators, who are
as childish as most people, have shaved, and
have had near shaves, with obsidian knives.

It is probable that the Minoan Empire had
a navy as well as a merchant marine.   Minos
was commonly represented as " Ruler of the
Waves," and the Greek historians, Herodotus
and Thucydides, refer to him as a mythical
character celebrated as the first possessor of a

Minos and the Minotaur

fleet. The extent of the Minoan Empire can be gauged by the survival of many trading stations and naval outposts on all the shores of the Ægean, from Sicily in the East to Gaza in the West, which bore the name " Minoa." There was a bad chapter, according to tradition, in the Empire's history. When the King's son Androgeos went to Athens to compete in the games, he won everything, and was killed in jealousy ; and the powerful Minos therefore decreed that seven Athenian boys and seven girls should be sent every nine years (or as other versions of the story say, every year) to be eaten by the Minotaur, a monster half man, half bull, which lived in the maze called the Labyrinth. That happened twice ; but on the third occasion the hero Theseus volunteered to go as one of the victims ; and with the aid of Ariadne, the King's daughter, who fell in love with him, he killed the monster. She gave him a sword and some string, which he fastened to the entrance of the maze as he went inside. He was thus able to find his way out again. Theseus had promised his father, the old King Ægeus, that if he returned alive, his ship would show white sails in place of the usual black, so that the news of his safety could be read in the distance. Whether in his elation or in his hurry to leave Naxos,

27

where (according to the story) he had deserted Ariadne, Theseus forgot his promise, and Ægeus, watching from the cliffs, and seeing that the sails were black, threw himself in despair into the sea. Hence the " Ægean " Sea. The discovery of Ariadne by the god Bacchus is the subject of a famous picture, now in the National Gallery, by Rubens.

Minos meanwhile reaped what he sowed. Dædalus, the architect of the Labyrinth, also fell a victim to the King's displeasure, and, making himself wings, fled to Sicily. His son Icarus, who went with him, flew too near to the sun ; the wax which fastened his wings melted, and he fell into the sea. Minos pursued Dædalus to Sicily, and was killed by treachery. His subjects went on a punitive expedition to the island, but never returned, and Crete was overrun by strangers.

That is legend. It is a fact, however, that the Minoan Empire did come to a sudden and violent end. Remnants of it—" the men from Keftiu " (" the Back of Beyond "), as the Egyptians called them—landed on the shores of Asia Minor, and finally settled in Palestine as the Philistines of the Bible. The mists of legend are clearing. The huge palace at Knossos is one of the solidest sights revealed. In its bewildering corridors, staircases, and

Minos and the Minotaur

rooms one recognizes the Labyrinth itself—a recognition which is confirmed by evidence disclosed within the palace.

In further excavation carried out in the early part of this year (1922) Sir Arthur Evans discovered what he describes as "the opening of an artificial cave, with three roughly-cut steps leading down to what can only be described as a lair adapted for some great beast." Lest fact should overleap itself into fable again, Sir Arthur adds :—"But here it is better for imagination to draw rein."

The stories of Minos and the Minotaur came to be regarded by classical Greece with something like awe. A ship, supposed to have been the one that took Theseus to Knossos, was preserved and was sent every year with special sacrifices to Delos. During its absence Athens was in a state of solemnity, and no acts were performed which were thought to involve a public stain. The execution of Socrates, for instance, was postponed thirty days till its return.

Chapter 4 : *Knossos*

"AND in Crete is Knossos, a great city, and in it Minos ruled for nine seasons, the bosom friend of mighty Zeus " (Homer, "Odyssey," xix. 178–179). Those "nine seasons " were long periods of varied activity. Ancient Crete was the home of an artistic, commercial and imperial people—there was a Minoan Empire—and Knossos, the capital of Crete, held the palace of Minos.

The Palace at Knossos was built on the slope of a low hill—the hill now known as " tou tselebe he kephala " or the Gentleman's Head—which overlooks a secluded valley, three and a half miles from the north coast of the island. It thus escaped the roving eye of passing pirates, and at the same time commanded a view, from a neighbouring hill, of the Minoan ships which lay beached in the harbour. That fleet was practically its only defence. Knossos had no wall of fortification. Like pre-war London she depended on her island security and on her command of the seas. She was not exposed, as were the mainland cities of Mycenæ and Tiryns, and as

Knossos

modern Paris, to the danger of invasion by land. The lack of fortification was one of the first points that struck the excavator. In his report of the first season's work (1900), Sir Arthur Evans says : " The extent and character of the outer walls are not yet apparent, but it is clear that while the compact castles of the Argolid were built for defence, this Cretan palace with its spacious courts and broad corridors was designed mainly with an eye to comfort and luxury " (*Journal of Hellenic Studies*, vol. xx, p. 168).

There were minor fortifications, chiefly near the north gate, consisting of a guard-house and bastions, but strategic considerations did not contribute to the main architecture at all.

It is an amazing structure. Built as long before Christ as the world has existed since Christ, it seems incredible that, for instance, it should have an underground drainage system. There is no doubt that Cretan architects were men of accomplishment. Mr. H. R. Hall says, in *The Ancient History of the Near East* (p. 47), that, " in comparison with this wonderful building (the later palace at Knossos), the palaces of Egyptian Pharaohs were but elaborate hovels of painted mud. Knossos seems to be eloquent of the teeming

31

life and energy of a young and beauty-loving
people for the first time feeling its creative
power."

The present ruins belong to three structures
built at different times. The first was built
in M.M.I, or before 2000 B.C., and was
burnt down towards the end of M.M.II (about
1700 B.C.). It was later (about 1600 B.C.)
rebuilt on a bigger scale, and this building in
its turn, after some three hundred years of use,
was remodelled and enlarged. Sir Arthur
Evans made an important discovery in his
1922 excavation, which proves that the Middle
Minoan III period was brought to a violent
end by a big earthquake (about 1600 B.C.).
He found some small houses overwhelmed by
huge blocks—" some about a ton in weight,
hurled some twenty feet from the Palace
wall by what could only have been a great
earthquake shock."

It is the last magnificent palace, built on
the ruins of 1600 B.C., that predominates in
to-day's ruins ; in it the Cretans reached the
height of their culture. This period, to which
belongs what is known as the " Palace Style "
in art, was as short-lived as it was brilliant.
Within fifty years (so the evidence seems to
show) the palace was raided and burnt, and
that was the end of Ancient Crete ; for the

same invaders who sacked Knossos also destroyed the palace at Phæstos.

It is lucky, however, that Minoan libraries were made not of paper, but of clay tablets. They were preserved, not destroyed, by the fire. The baking they then underwent enabled them to survive the dampness of the soil, and they remain to this day, a potential interpreter of much that is still obscure. They cannot yet be read. Scholarship has the hard but grateful task before it of discovering from these documents the Minoan language. It is lucky, again, that the sackers of Knossos had no use for clay tablets, which accordingly escaped the doom of more " valuable " loot. Dr. Burrows, in *The Discoveries of Crete* (p. 19), quotes in comment a Reuter telegram which, in reference to the fire at Seville in 1906, announced that " the archives were totally destroyed, but the cash and valuables were saved ! "

The outer walls of the palace were mainly built of gypsum, a stone composed of crystals of calcium sulphate, which is found plentifully around Knossos. It was so soft that it needed a covering of lime plaster to protect it against the weather. The exterior of the building, therefore, presented an expanse of white plaster, relieved perhaps in places by

33   c

The Minoans

decoration or colour. (See Noel Heaton on " Minoan Lime Plaster and Fresco Painting " in the *Journal of the Royal Institute of British Architects*, xviii, p. 697 (1911).) The palace was a square building covering about five acres, or as big an area as Buckingham Palace, and had a flat roof. In shape it was a hollow rectangle with a central court, measuring nearly two hundred feet from north to south, and not quite half as much in breadth, so that the encircling wings on the east and west were proportionately broader than the strip of buildings on the north and south. The bulk of the building was, in fact, divided up between these two wings, the one on the west standing higher up the hillside and having fewer storeys than the one on the east, whose foundations sloped down to the valley. Beyond the west wing there was another court —the meeting-place for the people of the town and the people of the palace ; and out to the north-west a smaller building—the Little Palace—connected with the palace proper by what Sir Arthur Evans has called " the oldest paved road in Europe," while a little to the north-east was the Royal Villa.

If you follow the course of this paved road as it approaches the Palace, you will see a

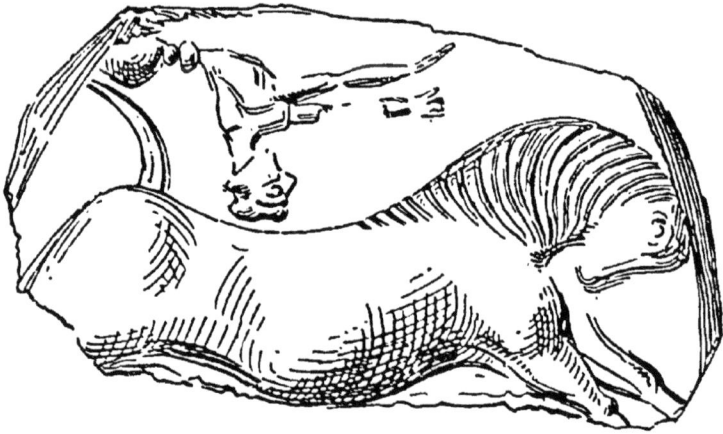

BULL LEAPING

From *The Annual of the British School at Athens*

small open space, forty feet by thirty, enclosed on two sides by rising tiers of steps with a raised platform in the corner between them. This was the theatre. Some scholars identify it with the dancing-place (choros) which, so tradition tells us, " Dædalus wrought in broad Knossos for fair-haired Ariadne " (Homer, " Iliad," xviii. 590) ; although Sir Arthur Evans thinks the choros was in a Palace Court. It would hold about 500 spectators, who made part or all of the " great throng that surrounded the lovely dancing-place, full of glee " (to quote the same tradition). No doubt the boxing contests and other forms of sport were held there. The Cretans, to judge by the pictures which have been discovered, were given to strenuous and exciting, possibly cruel, forms of sport. A painted panel depicts a bull-fighting scene. In it are two girls and a boy, the girls distinguished from the boy by their white skin, although all three wear the same sort of " cowboy " dress. A bull, head down, is charging one of the girls, who grips its horns in the attempt, apparently, to turn a somersault over its back, a feat which the boy is represented as in the process of accomplishing. He is half-way over, and the second girl stands ready to catch him. (See *Journal of Hellenic Studies*, xxiii, p. 381.

The Minoans

There is a copy of the fresco in the Ashmolean Museum, Oxford.)

Fifty yards to the east of the theatre is the northern entrance of the palace, which leads directly into the central court. Round this court are grouped the various rooms of the palace.

Chapter 5 : *Prehistoric Engineering and Architecture*

THE plan of the palace of Knossos is at first sight rather confusing, especially when one reflects that it represents only the ground floor of the original building and that one has to imagine, in some places two, and in others perhaps three storeys of rooms above it. If this is the old labyrinth of legend, no wonder, you think, that Theseus needed his Ariadne to show him a way out of it ; and that Dædalus, who built it, could himself find no other means of escape but by flying straight up into the air !

But it is the nature of legend to exaggerate ; and one can easily understand how, years after the destruction of the palace, the deserted ruins with their ghostly corridors and chambers would create the impression of an " inextricable maze " which was crystallized by tradition and became the setting for so many of the Cretan stories. As it stood in the days of Minos, the palace would not, of course, be anything so fantastic. The arrangement

37

The Minoans

of the rooms and corridors, though on a great
and elaborate scale, was based on a simple
plan. The mass of buildings in the west
wing of the palace is divided into two halves
by a long corridor running north and south,
those in the east wing by one running east
and west, and the four divisions thus made
fall into a regular scheme.

In the west corridor, which is four yards
wide and sixty-six yards long, there are still
standing some of the huge stone vases, " big
enough," as Sir Arthur Evans has said, " to
hide the Forty Thieves." They were used
for the storage of grain, oil, wine, dried fruits,
and the like. Opening on this corridor from
the west there is a series of magazines and
small chambers which were also used for
storage purposes ; while under the floors,
both of the magazines and of the corridor,
were strong cists, some of them lined with
lead, which would perhaps contain the State
treasures. The entrance which leads from
the west court or market-place, and which is
conveniently near the commissariat quarters,
would be used by tradesmen. Speaking of
the outer wall of the palace which borders on
the west court, the Haweses (*Crete the Forerunner of Greece*, p. 66) remark : " This
has a projecting base, whereon the peasants

38

CUPBEARER

From *The Discoveries in Crete*. By R. M. Burrows (John Murray)

[*To face page* 39

Prehistoric Engineering

and humbler merchants could sit dozing, with
one eye upon their merchandise and pack
animals. During the long morning hours
when traffic was busiest, this seat was always
in the shade—a pleasant refuge from the sun's
rays that beat so fiercely on the open court."
The low narrow ledge would not, however,
have been particularly comfortable to sit on.
In a narrow corridor to the west of the south
main entrance was found the fresco painting
of the Cupbearer, an astonishing work of art.
It portrays a Minoan youth, stiff with dignity,
carrying a gold and silver vase before him.
It did not originally stand in the corridor in
which it was found and to which it has given
its name, but on the west wall of the south
entrance. It fell into the corridor when the
connecting wall broke down. There is a repro-
duction of the Cupbearer on the cover of Dr.
Burrows's *The Discoveries in Crete*, which lacks,
of course, the brilliant colours of the original.

On the other side of the central corridor of
the west wing are the rooms in which State
and religious functions were held. In the
Throne Room, which is almost intact, the
magnificent throne of Minos is still standing,
carved out of solid stone, and along the wall
on each side of it are the stone benches on
which his counsellors sat. This would be the

chief room of the Minoan Government, in which foreign ambassadors were received and the affairs of State generally administered; important cases of justice would also be settled there, and Minos would be Supreme Judge. It will be remembered that Minos was not only the legislative head of a great sea empire. Being of divine origin himself, he is represented as a great Law-giver and Priest of Zeus, holding converse with the god every nine years in the Dictaean cave and receiving from him, like the Moses of the Old Testament, a famous code of laws which held good throughout the period of the Minoan Empire.

At his death, in accordance with the belief that men in the Lower World carried on the duties of their lifetime, he became a Judge of the Dead. Recounting his visit to the nether regions, Odysseus says : " Then I saw Minos, the famed son of Zeus, with his golden sceptre, dealing out justice to the dead, as he sat there ; and around him, their King, the dead asked concerning their rights, sitting and standing, in the wide-gated house of Hades " (Homer, "Odyssey," xi. 568 571).

Leaving the west wing of the palace and crossing the central court, you descend into the east wing by the Great Staircase which, even when found, was in a surprising state of

Prehistoric Engineering

preservation, and which by the end of 1910 had had the remains of no fewer than five flights restored to their original position. This staircase was traversed, as its discoverer said, "some three and a half millenniums back by kings and queens of Minos' stock, on their way from the scenes of their public and sacerdotal functions in the west wing of the palace to the more private quarters of the royal household." These quarters occupy the south-east corner of the palace, built on the slope of the hill and overlooking the valley. Approaching them from the central corridor which runs due east from the central court, you pass first through the men's halls—the Hall of the Colonnades and the Hall of the Double Axes—and thence by a dark crooked corridor, called from its shape the Dog's Leg Corridor, the effect of which was "to enhance the privacy of the rooms beyond," you come to the Queen's Megaron, and the ladies' apartments. A megaron was a sort of hall with columns across it, open at one end to let in the light. In other parts of the building, light was admitted by means of shafts sunk from the roof to the ground floor.

The queen's megaron is especially luxurious; it is decorated on a principle which, as Sir Arthur Evans says, was used

The Minoans

later by the Romans of the Empire. The wall paintings, done in perspective, included a scene of the sea with fishes playing, another of forest life, and a dado of dancing girls.

It was in this part of the building, too, that the drainage and water supply put the engineers on their mettle. This was the lowest part of the sloping hillside on which the palace stood, and the water supply, which came from the neighbourhood of the North Gate, had to be so organized as to prevent flooding—a stiff enough problem for engineers of 4,000 years ago. They solved it by a system of parabolic curves which subjected the flow to friction. Sinks, lavatories, underground pipes suggest modern drainage. They, nevertheless, were in use at Knossos.

The rooms of the building in this south-east part were arranged in terraces at different levels on the hillside. The fact of the grand staircase having five flights does not mean that there were five storeys one on top of the other. As a result of the final restoration of this staircase by Sir Arthur Evans and Dr. Mackenzie in 1910, it appears that " the upper landing of the fifth flight does not lead on to the ground floor of the central court, but answers in height to what must have been the first floor of the rooms on the other or western side. It must itself, therefore, have led on to some raised building, probably a terrace, that ran along the eastern side of the court" (*Britannia Yearbook*, 1913, " Crete," p. 269. Dr. R. M. Burrows).

There remains the north-east section. This was occupied by the artists and workmen of the palace. In one room olives were pressed, the oil being carried away by a conduit which turns twice at right angles till it reaches a spout set in the wall lower down the hill, more than fifty feet away. There the oil-jars were filled, and oil-jars are still standing in an adjoining room. Another room has been identified by the imagination of Sir Arthur Evans as the schoolroom. In other rooms pots were " thrown " and painted ; stone vases carved ; gold, silver, and bronze work moulded ; sculptures were chiselled ; seal stones and gems cut ; and the favourite miniatures in ivory were carved which, in a. compass of ten or eleven inches, reproduced a human form to the minutest detail of veins and finger-nails.

It will be seen, then, that the palace of Knossos was something more than the seat of King Minos. It contained a community completely organized within its walls, and independent of any outside connexion, after the manner of a mediæval castle.

Chapter 6 : *Internal Politics: the Relations of Knossos and Phæstos*

ON the other side of the island, at Phæstos, there was another great palace, which has been excavated by the Italian Archæological Mission. In many ways this palace was as magnificent as that of Knossos. Like Knossos, it was built on a hill on a foundation formed by levelling the buildings that had existed on the site from the Neolithic Age ; and, like Knossos, though on a smaller scale, it consisted roughly of a system of buildings grouped round a central court. Some of the remains are in a better state of preservation than those of Knossos and are, therefore, useful in supplementing our knowledge of the Golden Age of ancient Crete, which we chiefly derive from Knossos. It must be remembered, however, that owing to the architectural device of levelling the old buildings as foundations for the great palaces, both Knossos and Phæstos are of less value than the other sites in Crete, as

44

illustrating the Early Minoan Age—the period, that is, which preceded these great palaces.

There were, then, two great palaces flourishing in Crete during the same period. One naturally wonders what were the relations between them.

The established facts are few. It has been already shown, on the evidence of their respective pottery, that the original settlers at Phæstos came later than those of Knossos and took over the latter's ceramic innovations. The great palaces of the two cities were built about the same time, possibly (in view of the likeness in style) by the same architects. Both palaces were destroyed more than once, and at approximately known dates. These are the bare facts revealed by archæology, and the ice is thin for speculation on the internal politics of the island.

Some think, with the Haweses (*loc. cit.*, p. 70), that the first palace of Knossos was "attacked and burned at the close of the Second Middle Minoan period, *possibly by the rival ruler of Phæstos*." Yet the only certainty is that Knossos was burned down at that time and Phæstos was not.

Mr. H. R. Hall has a different impression. He says (*The Ancient History of the Near East*, p. 45) : "At the same time that the king

45

The Minoans

of Knossos built his new palace in his capital
. . . he also built himself a southern palace
in the Messarà. . . . As from the near neighbourhood of Knossos a fine view of the sea, the
haven, and the ships of the thalassocrats could
be obtained, with Dia beyond and perhaps
Melos far away on the horizon, so from Phais-
tos itself an equally fine, but different, prospect
greeted the royal eyes ; from this hilltop he
could contemplate on one side the snowy tops
of Ida and on the other the rich lands of the
Messarà." He thinks that before the palace of
Phæstos was built, the island, or at least the
central portion of it, had been unified under the
rule of Knossos. Legend makes Phæstos a
colony of Knossos.

An obviously important fact to be remembered in any discussion on this point is that,
in sharp contrast to the Mycenæan cities of
the mainland, Knossos and Phæstos were in
the main unfortified. It is true that M.
Dussaud has suggested that Knossos was
fortified, but the vast majority of scholars agree
that his supposed " fortifications " were nothing
of the kind. Dr. Burrows has devoted a
special chapter to this point in the as yet
unpublished revised edition of his book, the
manuscript of which he left in my care when he
died. His general conclusion is that, while

there may have been some sort of fortification in the early days of Crete, Knossos established a peaceful regime when she won her supremacy in L.M.I.   In any case, Knossos was not fortified in the days of her empire.   She had no fear from within the island, and she had command of the seas.

Chapter 7 : *Minoan Architecture and Fresco Painting*

PERHAPS the most vivid traces of the ancient civilization of Crete are the remains of the buildings which have been found in the soil. Here you have the rooms that were lived in, and the appeal to the imagination is direct. The relics of buildings are more extensive than those of any other kind, and they were the first discovered by the excavator, just as they are the first points of interest to the visitors who nowadays go to the island.

The buildings of the Stone Age have left hardly a trace of themselves, because they were made of such perishable materials as mud, reed, and wickerwork. Dr. L. Pernier has discovered, under the Minoan palace at Phæstos, a bit of the floor of one of these mud huts. It consists of red clay about four inches thick. Some houses, it is true, have been found near the modern Palaikastro, built of unhewn stone, and dating from the Neolithic Age, but they are exceptional. It was only when metal tools were invented that stone could be used generally for building. At the beginning of the Bronze Age the lower walls used to be made of stone, and the upper of sunburnt brick, the latter being further strengthened by wooden stays. Lime plaster was used even then to protect the walls against the weather. Later in the Bronze Age, when the great palaces were built, it became the practice to build foundations and lower walls to a height of about two yards of strong limestone blocks, some of them three yards long and one yard wide, and of gypsum. A protective covering of plaster was then applied. The upper storeys were generally of wood. Wood was extensively used. Professor Mosso, in reference to a wall of the vestibule at the top of the great staircase at Phæstos, says that "a base of alabaster having been made, holes were made in it to fix slabs of wood all round. These were bound together, and the hollow was filled with a mixture of lime and rubble" (*The Palaces of Crete*, p. 47). Whole tree-trunks were sometimes used as beams, and one can still see the holes in the stone into which they were fixed.

There are many features of these palaces which are worth minute study. In the building of the great palaces it was the practice to prepare the ground with a thick mixture of lime and clay and pebbles. This mixture set

The Minoans

so hard that it has now to be broken up with explosives before objects below can be removed. The staircase at Knossos measures nearly fifteen yards from side to side, and the steps are two and a half feet wide and hardly five inches deep. The most famous steps in Rome were not more than five and a half yards from side to side. The doors of the palace, of which there were many, were made to fit into the walls when open, so as not to interfere with corridor space. At Hagia Triada the drains of 4,000 years ago may still be seen working in wet weather. At Knossos the main drain, which had its sides coated with cement, was more than three feet high and nearly two feet broad, large enough for a man to move along it ; and the smaller stone shafts that discharged into it are still in position.

The water supply entered the palace from the north. In 1904 Sir Arthur Evans discovered some pipes in position to the north-west of the palace, running alongside the paved road which leads to the Theatral Area and the Little Palace. The necks of these pipes point eastward towards the palace and they lead from the very hills on the west from which the Venetian and Turkish aqueduct still supplies Candia. They must, therefore, have been aqueducts and not drains, and probably form part of the same system as the terra-cotta pipes discovered in the earlier excavations further east, and at the time considered to be connexions in the drainage system. They are thus described by Dr. Burrows : " Each of them was about two and a half feet long, with a diameter that was about six inches at the broad end, and narrowed to less than four inches at the mouth, where it fitted into the broad end of the next pipe. Jamming was carefully prevented by a stop-ridge, that ran round the outside of each narrow end a few inches from the mouth, while the inside of the butt, or broader end, was provided with a raised collar that enabled it to bear the pressure of the next pipe's stop-ridge, and gave an extra hold for the cement that bound the two pipes together " (*Ibid.*, p. 9).

There were also baths at Knossos. At any rate, a good many people think they were baths. Professor Mosso thinks they were chapels—a good instance of the excitement which attaches to archæological research. There is no arrangement, says Professor Mosso, for the supply or discharge of water, a provision which, he argues, is necessary for a bath ; moreover, the basin is lined with gypsum, which is soluble in water ; one of them was placed in the Throne Room ; and, finally, they were not private. Professor Mosso's subtle eye even detects an enclosure, which he maintains was not put there for spectators of the bath, but for a chapel choir. These are attractive arguments, but Dr. Burrows answers quite simply that (1) the gypsum argument is ruled out because it would be covered with plaster ; (2) terra-cotta tubs have been found close at hand, and the Knossians might quite well have been content with tubbing instead of plunging into a large tank that needed elaborate pipes ; (3) the bath in the Throne Room was used for ceremonial ablutions, for which little water would be needed ; and (4) no objects suggesting any cult (such as images or altars) have been found to show that these places were chapels.

Or take the lighting arrangements. There was a system of shafts used at Knossos, at Tylissos (a little palace a few miles west of Knossos), at Phæstos, and at Hagia Triada. The light came down vertically at the back of the room, where the roof had been left uncovered for the purpose, and the floor specially cemented to stand exposure to the weather. While Sir Arthur Evans speaks of the light " pouring in between the columns " in one place, and in another of its " stealing in in cooler tones," Dr. Burrows was of opinion that in the latter case the cooler tones were so cool that lamps had to be used. Many lamps have, in fact, been found there. Big marble-standard lamps have also been found, which probably held two or even four wicks ; one of them was found in a niche on a staircase at Tylissos.

The use of lime plaster on the outer walls gave an opportunity to the Minoan artists, who not only painted frescoes on them, but fashioned the plaster into relief. (See " Minoan Lime Plaster and Fresco Painting," by Mr. Noel Heaton, *Journal of the Royal Institute of British Architects*, vol. xviii, pp. 697–710.) " Fresco " paintings are made as soon as the initial setting of the plaster takes place, and while it is still wet. Brilliant colours were used—red ochre in the Early Minoan period (made by burning yellow clay), then yellow (from the natural clay) and black ; then blue, progressing from a pale greenish tint in Middle Minoan to a dark blue in Late Minoan. The cupbearer is an example of fresco painting, and the bull's head of high relief ; the fresco painters merely attempted an outline and wash of colour in two dimensions, not indicating shades or folds of drapery. The main difference between Cretan painting on wet plaster and Egyptian painting on fine white limestone is that the Cretan gives a more vivid impression of movement, and the Egyptian more detail. (See " The Relations

The Minoans

of Ægean with Egyptian Art," *Journal of Egyptian Archæology*, vol. i, pt. 3, July, 1914, pp. 197–205.) This is partly accounted for by the fact that Minoan painting was often done when the plaster was still wet.

There are many other sites in Crete which cannot be dealt with here—Gournia on the north coast, Palaikastro and others in the east, and Vrokastro. Their main importance lies in their bearing upon Minoan town-planning. Vrokastro has been explored by Miss E. H. Hall, who published her results in 1914 (*Anthropological Publications of the University of Pennsylvania.* Philadelphia). It has a special interest because it belongs to the Iron Age, and shows the inferiority of this age to its predecessor, the Bronze Age. In general, the houses in these towns were huddled together with the object of leaving as much ground as possible free for agriculture. They are poor specimens of houses,—small two-storeyed cottages with windows on each side of the door. Several rooms have been discovered in which upright faces of rock served as walls —a device still used in Crete. An interesting point about them is that they were built on rocky eminences or spurs of mountains—a significant sidelight on the fall of Knossos and the disappearance of her fleet.

Chapter 8 : *The Pottery*

" Exceeding lightly, as when some potter sits and tries
the wheel, well fitting in his hands, to see if it will run."—
HOMER.

CRETE is the only land of the " prehistoric " Near East which has left no
record of itself besides that revealed by
excavation. And even the writing on the
clay tablets cannot yet be read. We none
the less get a vivid impression of Cretan life
on its artistic side, and for this the main credit
is due to the unique value of pottery in archæology. Pottery is almost indestructible.
While it may decompose in soil that is damp
enough, and the design may be obliterated
when fire plays on it directly and when there
is enough air for oxidization, yet the actual
fabric, being made originally of clay baked
hard by extreme heat, can never be destroyed
by fire. It cannot rust. It cannot be pounded
into dust, because a small sherd has a tremen-
dous power of resistance. While the stone
ruins at Knossos will one day vanish from
exposure to the weather, the pottery will
remain. The defects of pottery are as valuable

55

to the archæologist as its qualities. Its brittle-
ness led to a constant deposit of breakages.
The replacing of breakages in what was a
household necessity led to continuous pro-
duction. Its cheapness made it valueless to
looters. When palaces were raided and burnt,
metal objects were " lifted " either for their
actual value or their potential value in
the melting-pot. The pots remained.
Thousands of sherds have been found on
every site in Crete. Even when fragments
cannot be pieced together, they reveal the
kind of clay, decoration and thickness of the
original vase, and complete examples are
often found in tombs, where they were placed
as tributes to the dead, in accordance with an
almost universal custom in early Greek civilization.

The evidence thus obtained has many
uses. It shows the consecutive development
of pottery as a form of art, in itself interesting,
and the corresponding changes in the taste
of the people. As the art progresses, we find
vases, for instance, with scenes painted on them
illustrating contemporary customs, methods of
burial, religious rites, styles of dress and
buildings. The prehistoric pottery of Crete
never reached this stage, but even so, it
supplies the bulk of the evidence on which the

The Pottery

Minoan civilization is being reconstructed.

Pottery has been the chief instrument, too, in the formulation of a system of dating. By assuming a lapse of a thousand years for every yard of deposit—except in the Stone Age, when the accumulation of debris was quicker, because huts were built of ephemeral material such as mud and wickerwork—each successive layer is relatively dated according to its depth from the surface. Pots provide the nucleus for this scheme, being found in large numbers in every layer. Other objects take their place according to the type of pots they are found with. Not that the process is simple. There are complicating factors, and even pottery creates difficulties and irregularities. At Knossos, for instance, when the first palace was built, the top of the hill was levelled and a portion of the former deposit thus cut away. Obviously, too, heirlooms would belong to an earlier time than that of the layer in which they are found. Or a pot may be displaced in the earth. A safeguard, however, against mistakes is afforded by the abundance of pots, which makes the differentiation of general classes easy.

Pots, then, are found at the lowest levels, just above virgin soil, for the earliest people used them and broke them. The slowness

The Minoans

of development in that long-drawn-out period (the Neolithic or Later Stone Age) is clearly indicated. There are some seven yards of deposit belonging to it at Knossos, and the latest ware shows little or no improvement on the first. The pottery is hand-made, the clay coarse, generally of a sooty-greyish colour and more or less burnished. The relics consist of the rims and handles of pots, rims of basins, bowls, and plates and similar fragments, too incomplete to suggest original shapes. Two interesting points, however, can be seen. The pots were hand-polished both inside and out, and incised lines, or lines simply scratched on the surface, were used as ornamentation. This primitive manifestation of an artistic impulse was later extended by the filling of the incised lines with a white substance for greater effect. Similar ware has been found at Troy and in Egypt, and Dr. Mackenzie has thought that these were an importation from the Ægean (*Journal of Hellenic Studies*, vol. xxiii, p. 159).

The irresistible impulse manifested even in primitive people to decorate their ordinary vessels is further illustrated by the fact that the polishing was gradually heightened, and the glitter thrown into relief by ripples, made with a blunt instrument, probably bone, and

The Pottery

suggestive of the ripples on the surface of water. Among the latest Neolithic ware found at Knossos are two remarkable specimens of incised ware, the design being that of a twig with leaves. On each side of the stem is a row of small oblong punctuated points, filled in with white chalk. This, it must be remembered, in a period which ended about 3000 B.C.

The Bronze Age, which followed, and which brought with it the Minoan period at Knossos, is remarkable for the first use of paint. The transition was gradual and slow, and indeed, at the beginning of the Bronze Age, there is a falling off in the quality of the pottery. This was due to an interesting result of the discovery of metal, which turned the attention of skilled artists to the new medium, and left the fashioning of stone and clay to inferior hands. On the manufacturing side, however, it is probable that a great step forward was taken at that time. The fact that the clay is now of a terra-cotta or brick colour, as opposed to the former peaty grey of Neolithic times, has led to the surmise that the potter's kiln was now used for baking.

The first paint invented was an almost lustreless black, which was developed gradually into a lustrous black. Even this development

was at first used as a mere imitation of the
Neolithic black hand-polished vases. The
paint was applied all over the vase, inside as
well as outside, whenever the neck was wide
enough. Neolithic incisions again were imi-
tated by white geometric patterns painted over
the black background. This style was not
usual till the end of the Early Minoan period
(E.M.III).

It was not till the beginning of the Middle
Minoan period that any serious development
took place. Then, however, it came in leaps.
The potter's wheel had been introduced,
probably from Egypt, at the end of Early
Minoan I, and henceforth pots were " thrown "
precisely as they are to-day. One can imagine
the keenness with which this great if simple
invention was exploited. The fashioning of
clay with thumb and fingers on a rotating
wheel led so easily and inevitably to fineness
of technique that the potter was soon imitating
the thinness of metal, and by the end of Middle
Minoan II was producing " egg-shell " vases.
In design the angular geometric patterns had
been displaced by the end of the Early Minoan
period by curves and spirals, the logical out-
come of the use of a brush. Colour meanwhile
became lavish and brilliant. There were two
styles : either the whole pot was first painted

The Pottery

black to provide a background for a light design, or a dark design was painted on the original light-coloured clay. It was the first of these styles that naturally lent itself to colour display, and the name " polychrome " (" many-coloured ") has been given to it. The other style (monochrome, or one-coloured) relied for its effect on a simple black-and-white contrast. In the latter case the light natural background was improved by a fine buff clay " slip " or wash. Quite naturally it was the polychrome style that mostly exercised the artists at first. Bright orange, lustreless white, yellow, red, crimson on a black background were exploited to a sometimes fantastic extent as long as the novelty of colour lasted.

The next development took place in the second Middle Minoan period (M,M.II). Relief was then introduced, which created an effect of light and shade on the black varnish. Mere blobs of colour, which constituted the original form of relief, soon developed into raised lumps and horns (the so-called " Barbotine " ware). Middle Minoan " Kamares " (so called because the first specimens were found by Professor Myres in a cave on the slope of Mount Ida above the village of Kamares), or polychrome pottery, chiefly consisted of cups, " tea-cups," jugs, amphoræ

61

The Minoans

(or two-handled jars), and fruit-stand vases.
The three best specimens are here reproduced.
In the Middle Minoan II period large storage
jars, or "pithoi," made their first appearance.
They were as big as a man, and almost exactly
like the Cretan storage jars of to-day. Two
interesting features in the decoration of these
jars are cunningly practical in origin. One
was an imitation in relief of the coils of rope
which were used in moving the jars, the other
a "trickle" ornament produced by allowing
splashes of paint to trickle down the side of
the jar—a device which made a virtue, in
anticipation, of the inevitable trickles which
would result from the storage of oil in it.

Towards the end of the Middle Minoan
period the exaggerated use of colour which
had marked the first introduction of polychrome ware gave way to a concentration
upon design. Perhaps the most remarkable
specimen of this later phase is the "lily vase"
found at Knossos. It stands about two feet
high, and for design has a simple row of lilies
painted in white on a purple ground. The
shape of the vase is artistically made to serve
the design by enabling the lilies to bend
slightly outward and then curve in a little at
the top.

Then came a curious clash in the separate

62

POLYCHROME CUPS

The Pottery

evolution of polychrome and monochrome ware. The latter had been used as an easy decoration for ordinary vessels, but towards the end of the Middle Minoan period the two styles began to coalesce in the form of a simple light design on a dark ground. Then a final resolution took place by a " volte face " into a monochrome dark on light brought about by the experience that the black varnish was a more durable colour than the lustreless colour pigments. The varnish, indeed, possessed a remarkable tenacity. It probably was the forerunner of that used in the later Attic Black Figure vases, whose secret still exercises the ingenuity of modern potters. As yet nothing further has been established than that the varnish was not a " glaze " in the modern sense. A contributing factor to the final triumph of the monochrome over polychrome rested upon simple necessity. When naturalist motives became dominant in the painter's art, the lack of a green pigment left no satisfactory alternative to the general abandonment of variation in colour. In Late Minoan I, when the complete absorption of the polychrome into the monochrome style took place, we find a general use of a brilliantly lustrous brown-to-black " glaze " paint on a buff clay slip, carefully polished by hand on

63

terra-cotta clay. The naturalism of plants and flowers now extends to sea-objects—fish, shells, weeds, rocks—and is marked by careful truth to life. A striking example of this style is a famous " octopus " vase found at Gournia.

As the rise of Cretan civilization had been faithfully reflected in pottery, so was its fall. One can trace in it the general decadence of Crete. In the eventful Late Minoan II period, which saw the final destruction of Knossos and the sudden end of Cretan greatness, the pottery becomes stiff and grandiose. Plants and animals are rendered in a spiritless, conventionalized manner. Degeneration was rapid, and in Late Minoan III, which represented the last stage of Minoan culture, the potter held his brush quite still and let the spinning pot do the rest. There was no decoration beyond an occasional group of horizontal bands, the mere framework of earlier designs.

There were, of course, other forms of pottery besides vases. Cretan potters, even more than those of to-day, used clay as the material for hardware. Not only bricks, drain-pipes, ornaments, but lamps, kettles, even cupboards and tables, were made of clay.

Chapter 9: *The Origin of Writing*

THE Cretans had a system of writing as long ago as 2500 B.C. The language therein embodied is still a mystery to us, in spite of Sir Arthur Evans's monumental work *Scripta Minoa* (1909). The hope is that Sir Arthur will find a clue to the mystery, but up to the present the fact is that there is no starting-point for any attempt at interpretation. If a bilingual inscription could be found—a Cretan document, that is, side by side with a translation in some known language such as Egyptian—a start could be made.

It was inevitable that the art of writing should be evolved early in the history of man. Even in the most primitive stages of life there would be the elementary necessity, for instance, of identifying one's own property, and for this the most likely means would be some system of marking. Then, again, the development of communal life would entail the duty of keeping appointments, or of doing a particular thing at a particular time. It would, one thinks, have been too much of a strain, even for the

The Minoans

mind of a Stone Age man, to keep all the details of his daily, still more of his annual, routine in his head, and the handkerchiefs of those remote days may not have been of such a material as to lend themselves readily to mnemonic knots. It is quite conceivable, as an instance of the sort of necessity that would arise, that at a given time it could be calculated how many days ahead the provisions would last, and when, therefore, the hunter must be ready for the hills. He might prepare a handy reminder with a pictographic representation of some commonplace event that was to take place at the same time, and by hanging the picture up in an obvious spot.

One's range of activity would increase as time went on, and it might conceivably be necessary to deliver a message to a man over on the other side of the valley in circumstances where one could not take it oneself. Such a contingency would produce some form of written message, for the message might be private or unsuitable for oral transmission by a third party. To give a concrete example from later times : Proitus wanted to kill Bellerophon, but did not want to do it himself ; he therefore sent the doomed man to the King of Lycia " with letters of introduction written on a folded tablet, containing much ill against

66

the bearer . . . that he might be slain "
(Homer, " Iliad," vi. 169). Not all people
are original enough to transmit such a com-
munication orally by the bearer.

Fifty, even forty, years ago it was the general
doctrine of Greek scholars that the Homeric
poems were never written down till long after
they were composed, perhaps even, so some
thought, not until 560 B.C. Till then, we used
to be taught, they were preserved wholly by
memory and by oral transmission. But on the
strength of the above passage from Homer—
the only passage in either " Iliad " or " Odyssey " where writing is mentioned—Andrew
Lang in 1883 argued that the art of writing
must have been known to the early Greeks.
" It is almost incredible," he said, " that the
quick-witted Greeks should have neglected an
art which met them everywhere in Egypt and
Asia." He argued better than he knew. Not
only was the art of writing known to the early
Greeks, but it was known to their forerunners
a few thousand years earlier, forerunners whose
very existence was not suspected when Andrew
Lang wrote. Curiously there had been found
no trace of writing in the Mycenæan remains,
although this fact has since been shown to be
due to mere chance.

In 1893 Sir (then Mr.) Arthur Evans caused

The Minoans

general astonishment by communicating to the Hellenic Society his discovery of the fact that certain seal stones which he had found in Greece, and which had been assumed to be Peloponnesian, were, in fact, Cretan. This startling revelation was clinched during the years that followed by the discovery of further specimens of Cretan writing. Excavation in Crete was started in 1900, and the first year's work yielded up hundreds of clay tablets inscribed with Cretan writing. Was Homer writing fairy stories when he made Proitus send his doomed Bellerophon to Lycia with his " folded tablet " ? Or did he know that the Lycians were colonists from Crete ?

A tentative sketch of the successive phases through which the art of writing passed may be made, even if it largely depends upon unconfirmed surmise. The temptation to fill in the gaps by what seems reasonable conjecture is hard to resist.

Minoan writing must have started, quite naturally, with simple pictographs, such as have, in fact, been found—simple pictures of a man, a leg, a ship, representing a definite thing that it was desired to indicate. They are called " ideographs " because they signify a single idea. They next developed into " hieroglyphs," that is, pictures which had

The Origin of Writing

acquired by association a certain use among the people who employed them, but whose original meaning has been lost, and can now only be inferred. In the parallel case of Egyptian hieroglyphics, guessing at such meanings has been shown to be dangerous work, for in many cases the established interpretation is far other than what one might have supposed.

The first pictographs were evolved in the Early Minoan period (c. 2800–2600 B.C.), and are found on seal stones. It may be fairly assumed, therefore, that in Crete the first method of writing down ideas was by seal impressions. By the Middle Minoan period the seal stones are elongated, and contain a succession of designs, by which a connected chain of ideas could be reproduced. The lines of pictures are sometimes read from left to right, sometimes from right to left, a feature in which, as in others, they resemble the Hittite system of writing. In all cases the document is read in the direction in which the figures it contains are facing. *Scripta Minoa* (p. 203) gives a typical example of this species : namely, a picture of a ship with two crescent moons, of which the probable meaning was a voyage of two months' duration.

The next step in the evolution of writing

came, no doubt, when phonetic values were assigned to the pictures ; that is, when the sound made in pronouncing the name of a given thing or person or action became associated with the conventional ideograph which represented that thing or person or action. When that happened, the same ideograph began to be used in writing out other, more complex, words in which the same *sound* occurred, although in *meaning* there was no connection with the original pictograph. To take a hypothetical example. Suppose we were in that stage of evolution to-day. We may have formed the habit of denoting an axe by a simple picture of that instrument ; thereafter the sign of an axe would have become a symbol for spelling the same sound whenever it appeared in any other word. In spelling the word " accident," for instance, we should start with the picture of an axe. This sort of thing seems to us mere " punning," but it would cause no more difficulty or hesitation to the primitive writer than it would have, say, to Mr. Weller, senior, to whom the relation of the written to the spoken word and of words to things was still mysterious. Once begun, the method would be eagerly applied to fresh words.

The first attempt at " syllabics," or the

The Origin of Writing

writing out of a word by separate symbols for
its separate syllables, was made more intelligible
by the use of " determinatives." By " deter-
minative " is meant a pictographic representation of the idea denoted by the whole word.
These we find appended to the spelling of a
word in order to give the reader at least some
inkling as to whether the word denoted mineral,
animal or vegetable. A man's name, for
instance, would be followed by a picture of a
man.

The physical strain involved in drawing
pictures every time one wanted to write down
a word or two would obviously soon become
intolerable. It is not therefore to be wondered
at that, by the time of the Middle Minoan III
period, the hieroglyphics have been simplified
into conventional signs which are easier to
make. Herein is the germ of what we call
" linear " script, that is, of a system of writing
based on a set of regular forms, such as our
own alphabet. By the Late Minoan I period
there was a full linear script in use throughout
Crete, and it was extended to Melos and Thera.
Sir Arthur Evans has called this script " Class
A " to distinguish it from a parallel form of
it which was introduced in the next period
(Late Minoan II), and which he calls " Class
B." The latter is not a different script, but

The Minoans

merely a variation introduced, it is supposed, by a new dynasty at Knossos. Most of the Knossian tablets that have come down to us belong to the " Palace period," and are written in the Class B style.

It was the usual practice to write the inscriptions with a stilus, that is a pointed rod of metal, on a clay tablet, and this is the form of most of the inscriptions that have been preserved. It is possible that wooden tablets covered with a layer of wax were also used ; but even if they were, none of them, of course, could have survived the burning of the palaces. More interesting still is the fact that pen and ink must have been used even in those remote times. This fact is established by the discovery of two cups (Middle Minoan III) which are inscribed in ink. There can be little doubt, therefore, that long documents and any literature there happened to be were written in ink on papyrus. It is probable that we shall have to make up our minds to the complete loss of all such literature, for Cretan soil lacks the dryness of the Egyptian. If our worst fears prove true, we may experience the final anti-climax of the discovery that the clay tablets, when read, will contain nothing after all but lists and bills.

It is obvious that many of the tablets do

The Origin of Writing

consist of bills or inventories. Although we cannot yet understand the language of the script, it has been found possible, by studying the clay tablets, to reconstruct the system of numbers that was used. We have, for instance, what is evidently an inventory of arrows, a record surmounted by a picture of an arrow. From this and other records it is apparent that thousands were expressed by "diamonds," hundreds by slanting lines, tens by circles, units by straight lines, quarters by a small " v." The highest number recorded is 19,000.

Although it is true that scholars still wait a clear starting-point for transcribing the Cretan script, there is one interesting and important point already established by Sir Arthur Evans. He has proved to the general satisfaction of classical scholars that the Phœnician alphabet, which had always been supposed to be the original source of the Greek alphabet, and there-fore of the Latin alphabet from which comes our own, was itself derived from Crete. This theory, however, is disputed by Egyptologists.

There are in existence three fragmentary inscriptions, two of which were found not long ago by Professor R. C. Bosanquet at Præsos, in Crete—near to Mount Dicte, and not far to the north-east of the boundaries of Knossos —which are written in Greek characters, and

The Minoans

are therefore quite legible to us, but which contain a language which is not Greek. Is it the language of the Minoans? It is not yet possible to say, although Professor Conway, who has examined the inscriptions at length in the *Annual of the British School at Athens* (vol. viii, p. 125, and vol. x, p. 115), may some day be able to give an answer.

Chapter 10 : *Cretan Religion*

CRETAN religion differed from that of classical Greece in that the chief deity worshipped was a goddess, Mother Nature or Earth-Mother, some at least of whose characteristics we find embodied in the Rhea of Greek mythology. Matriarchal religion seems to have been specially characteristic of very early times ; through it primitive man expressed his veneration of womanhood. The Cretan Mother Goddess held an exalted position. She had supreme power over all Nature ; was associated with doves, which symbolized her power in the air ; was accompanied by lions, the strongest animals of the earth ; brandished snakes, that live under the earth. Among the various " cult objects," or ritualistic forms used in worship, that have been found in her shrines are included representations of cows with calves, goats with suckling kids, and the like.

There was a god as well as a goddess in Minoan religion, but he was of relatively little importance. Velchanos, the Cretan Zeus—if we may assume that the Minoan god was the

original of this figure of the Greek legends—
was represented as both the son and the hus-
band of Mother Nature. He was suckled, so
the tradition ran, by Amalthea the goat in the
cave of Dikte, and brought up by his mother
Rhea on the slopes of Mount Ida. His
insignificance in comparison with the goddess
appears from the fact that he was drawn on a
smaller scale whenever represented in her com-
pany. The two deities probably constituted,
as Mr. Hogarth has suggested, a " Double
Monotheism "—a double godhead, that is,
worshipped to the exclusion of all minor deities.
If this was the case, the various Cretan proto-
types of later Greek divinities must be regarded
as variant forms of the Mother Goddess herself.
Aphrodite, for instance, the goddess of Love,
was worshipped generally in the Levant, being
known in Canaan as Ashtaroth-Astarte, and in
Egypt as Hathor ; her Cretan name is unknown. The Greek Artemis, goddess of the
Wild Beasts, was foreshadowed in the Cretan
Dictynna.

One great difference between the Cretan
and the Hellenic Zeus was that the Cretan
Zeus was mortal, and was said to have died
on Mount Juktas. The mortality of their
gods was one of the striking conceptions which
differentiated the Southern peoples of the Near

Cretan Religion

East from the later Greeks, who came from the North. The Egyptian Osiris, for instance, could die, but not any of the Greek gods. The Cretan Mother Goddess is depicted on seal stones and rings dressed like an earthly queen, while Velchanos is seen descending from the heavens to the earth, a young warrior with a spear and an enormous shield.

Another difference between Cretan and classical Greek religion was that, as far as one can see, Cretan religion did not give rise to any great temples, nor left behind any more substantial traces of its activity than the small figures of the Earth Goddess to whom I have referred. It may be sound to regard the palace of Knossos as itself a temple, and it is true that legend makes of Minos a High Priest as well as a King. There seems, however, to be little room for doubt that the only places set aside specifically for worship were small private shrines used for family worship. All the evidence tends to indicate that it was the family idea that predominated in Cretan worship. Private houses had their shrines, and the Knossian palace-temple itself had its lesser family shrines. These sanctuaries were always distinguished by a sort of sacred pillar, a sign which in Minoan art is often used as the only indication of a sacred place. There is an

77

example of it on a fresco painting found at Knossos. Another emblem associated with the cult is that of sacred trees, which on rings and seal stones usually form the background for the " choros," or dance. The actual dance, no doubt, would be performed in sacred groves.

Many cult-objects have been found in the shrines, the commonest being the mysterious Double Axe. The fact that this emblem was also specially associated with the Carian Zeus at Labraunda has led to a generally accepted theory that the Cretan " Labyrinth " corresponds to the Carian " Labraunda," or place of the " Labrus " or Double Axe ; for the Knossian palace must have been, in fact, the chief seat of the cult.

Side by side with the Double Axe one finds the constantly-recurring sign of the Bull, an animal which was sacred not only because of its physical strength, but of its use in sacrifice. A sarcophagus or coffin of terra-cotta, found at Hagia Triada, contains a picture of a sacrificial bull following a procession of women priests. In view of the prominence given to the Bull in Minoan worship, one need not seek far for an explanation of the Cretan legend of the Minotaur, a monster half man, half bull, which lived in the labyrinth and exacted its human victims. Nor is it impossible that

78

Cretan Religion

the dangerous and cruel sport of bull-fighting formed part of the same cult. Bulls' heads were made in pottery, and sometimes of gold, and used as votive offerings. The horns of the bull—Horns of Consecration—are found in shrines among ritual objects.

Cult-objects were usually of a rude and inartistic kind. A striking exception is found in some brilliantly-coloured figures of ware which if it were modern would be called "faïence," belonging to the Middle Minoan III period. Perhaps the best example of this ware is a group consisting of the Snake Goddess and her votaries, which was found by Sir Arthur Evans in 1903, and which was used in a shrine of the royal household.

There was a specially important element in Cretan religion reserved for the cult of the dead.

It is obvious from the many tombs that have been excavated, that in very early times it was the practice to bury the body of the dead in a doubled-up position, the knees being drawn up to the breast. In later times the body was laid out at full length. It is not clear whether or not there was any particular significance in this choice of position. There were various kinds of tombs and graves, all of which were used contemporaneously, and of which, perhaps,

the most interesting were the "Tholoi."
The word "tholos" properly means a domed
building or rotunda, and the particular kind
of tomb to which it is applied is a vaulted
chamber to which entrance is effected through
an underground tunnel, or "dromos." It is
likely that in form these "tholoi" were based
upon the huts used—at some period—by the
living. There are both round and square
"tholoi" found in Crete. The "tholos" of
Hagia Triada has a circular ground plan, while
the Royal Tomb at Isopata and other elaborate
tombs of the great palace-periods are rect-
angular. The principle of the tholos-tomb
was most in use in Mycenæan times, on the
mainland of Greece, where the "beehive
tombs" almost all retained in the original
round formation. The hilly character of
Crete led the people to cut out their "tholoi"
in the side of the rocky hills, the "dromos," or
tunnel, in this case being driven into the hillside almost horizontally.

Another style of grave was the shaft or pit-
grave, which consisted of a pit sunk into the
ground, at the bottom of which was the grave
itself, closed over with slabs of stone. Still
another kind was a combination of the first
two, and is known as the "pit-cave." This
was made by first sinking a pit and then cutting

out the tomb in the form of a side-recess from the bottom of the pit. A simpler form of burial, known as the " pot-burial," was effected by trussing up the body, placing it under an inverted jar, and then burying it in the earth. A sixth form was that of the simple grave, like our own. Cremation was not practised in Minoan times, although it was introduced into Crete from Greece in the Iron Age. Clay coffins were first used in the Middle Minoan period, being made in the form of deep boxes with sloping tops resembling the roofs of houses.

Such were the physical conditions of burial. We knew practically nothing of the cult of the dead until 1913–1914, when Sir Arthur Evans published some important disclosures (*Archæologia*, 2nd series, vol. xv, 1913–14). It was known before that the dead in their spacious tombs were honoured with gift-offerings, which included weapons, jewellery, and objects closely associated with them in their life ; that food and drink offerings were made and coal fires lighted, possibly with the naïve or symbolic object of cheering the traveller on his mysterious way. Now, however, a new series of tombs has been found at Isopata, one of which, called by Sir Arthur Evans " the Tomb of the Double Axes," is proved to be

not only a tomb, but a shrine of the Minoan
Great Mother. In this tomb were found
libation vessels, including a " rhyton " (or
drinking-cup) in the shape of a bull's head
made of steatite, and a pair of double axes ;
the grave which received the body is cut out
in the form of a double axe. " The cult of
the dead," says Sir Arthur Evans, " is thus
brought into direct relation with the divinity
or divinities of the Double Axes, and we may
infer that in the present tomb the mortal
remains had been placed in some ceremonial
manner under divine guardianship."

Chapter 11 : *Men and Women, Clothes and Customs*

WHEN Knossos fell, Crete ceased to be the pre-eminent power in the Near East. The island itself was overrun by military or naval adventurers, and the centre of Mediterranean life shifted over to the mainland of Greece, whence, indeed, those adventurers came. The interesting thing, however, was that Cretan culture went with it, and neither for the last, nor probably for the first, time " the captive led captive her savage conqueror," as Horace wrote centuries afterwards. Crete stooped to conquer Greece, just as Greece in her turn stooped to conquer Rome.

The Cretans as a race were quite distinct from the contemporary inhabitants of Greece, physical types being sharply divided by the shores of the mainland. It may be asked : Is it worth while speculating about the physical characteristics of a people which flourished 4,000 years ago, whose very existence was obscured by the Dark Age that comes before Greek history, and whose existence was not

The Minoans

rediscovered until the other day? Yet archæology works wonders. It is true that in this particular field, in which archæology is chiefly dependent upon portrait-paintings and bones, there is more controversy and less certitude than in the others ; and that craniology, or the study of skulls, with their much-disputed classification into "brachycephalic" or broadheaded, "dolichocephalic" or long-headed, and "mesocephalic," midway between the two, is a fruitful source of confusion ; that the "cephalic" index—that is, the breadth of the skull above the ears expressed in a percentage which gives the proportion of this breadth-measurement to the measurement of the length of the same skull from the forehead to the occiput—is a poor index of anything at all. Still, there is ground for assuming that from the later Stone Age onwards the islands of the Ægean were mainly peopled by members of the "Mediterranean" race, small of stature, with oval faces, with what craniologists might call rather "long" heads, with small hands and feet, a dark complexion, dark eyes and black curly hair.

According to Professor H. L. Myres in his *Dawn of History*, the north-west quadrant of the Old World resolved itself racially into three belts, which were determined by geo-

graphical conditions. (Pp. 39 *et seq.* Williams
& Norgate, 1912.) In the north were the
pure white-skinned " Boreal " men of the
Baltic basin ; next came the sallow " Alpine "
type, then the red-skinned " Mediterranean "
man. The third was an intruder from the
South, not from far enough south for him to
be a negro, but probably from the northern
shores of Africa. His intrusion " formed part
of a much larger convergence of animals and
plants from the south and south-east into the
colder, moister regions which have been
released since the Ice Age closed." The
limit of the movement seems to have been
fixed by the shores of the mainland, further
north than which the lungs and constitution
of the people concerned forbade them to go.

The establishment of the existence of the
Mediterranean race has had, among other
results, that of making it no longer possible,
as was invariably the practice before Crete was
excavated, of ascribing all obscure factors in
the beginnings of Greece to a Phœnician
origin. We now know, for instance, that the
art of writing came from Crete, Phœnicia
being the medium ; and that Phœnicia itself
was merely a late centre of the general Ægean
civilization, and got its name merely because
it was the best-known branch of the " red-

The Minoans

skinned " race ; for " Phœnikes " literally
means " Red-skins," and in Homer Phœnix
himself is a King of Crete and grandfather of
Minos.

The Minoan people, then, formed part of
the Mediterranean race. Their dress was
much simpler than that of the classical Greeks.
The men wore a short pair of drawers or a
loin-cloth, the upper part of the body being
bare, as in the cupbearer picture, a style
emanating, as did the men themselves, from
the warm lands south of the Mediterranean.
Egyptian fresco-paintings reveal an almost
exact analogy of type in the clothing and
appearance of the Egyptians. Those who
have a keen eye for the persistence of type
may compare some of the forms of loin-cloth,
as depicted on seal stones, with the " brakais,"
or baggy breeches, still worn in Crete. Elders
and officials apparently wore flowing cloaks for
their greater dignity. High-topped boots—
again suggestive of those worn to-day—were
in general use. Men wore their hair long as
did the women, plaited and coiled up on the
top of the head, thereby forming the only head-
dress that was used.

Minoan war-equipment was limited. Their
only weapons were a long sword and a dagger,
the latter of which is shown by pictures of clay

figurines to have been carried inside the belt at the front. Their only defensive armour was a big shield of leather and a leather conical helmet. The shield was framed in a metal band, but had no handle or central boss ; it was big enough to cover the body from head to foot, and it could be bent so as to protect both sides. It is represented in certain pictures in a curious 8-shape, pinched-in in the middle. The origin of this may have been that it was the practice to sling it over the left shoulder suspended by a strap, and for this purpose the figure-of-eight shape may have been convenient.

Horses were apparently used both for war and for hunting, although we have no pictures of them being ridden. The available evidence shows them only in the shafts of two-wheeled chariots. This accords well with Professor Sir William Ridgeway's observation (made far back in the 'eighties of last century) that in Homer the horse was driven only, and was no bigger than our donkey. There is reason for thinking that the horses were imported, and imaginative people have recognized evidence of this in the fact that a seal stone has been found which shows a horse on board ship. Whether intentionally or merely from crudity of draughtsmanship, one is left in little doubt

The Minoans

as to what mostly occupied the artist's mind when he fashioned this stone, for the horse covers three-quarters of the ship's length, and towers high above it, while the crew stand as high as the horse's knees. On the fascinating subject of the history of the horse, the reader should consult Sir W. Ridgeway's *Origin of the Thoroughbred Horse* (Cambridge University Press, 1905).

The women are readily distinguishable from the men in Cretan pictures by reason of their white skin, suggestive of a more secluded indoor life. They wore large shady hats, close-fitting, puffed-sleeved blouses, cut very low in front, and projecting upwards into a sort of peak at the back of the neck. They wore wide-flounced, richly-embroidered skirts like crinolines, and had belts like the men's. It was on first seeing some of the pictures of them that a French scholar compared the women of Knossos with those of Paris.

Minoan women enjoyed a far more " advanced " status than did other primitive women. In the art of their day they are represented as appearing in public and unveiled ; they took part in the bull-fighting at Knossos, and their apartments in the palace were marked out by their special luxury. The greatest glory for an Athenian woman of a later age was to be " as little mentioned as possible among men." Not so for the women of Crete. There may be some special significance in the fact that the Lycians of Asia Minor, who were colonists from Crete, made a practice of calling children by the mother's, not the father's, name (Herodotus, i. 73). If this was the case also in Minoan Crete itself, it may afford a possible explanation of the freedom enjoyed by Cretan women, for the practice of naming children after their mother instead of after their father is connected with states of society which have not yet evolved any definite ideas of marriage, and in which, as Herbert Spencer says, " The connection between mother and child is always certain, whereas the connection between father and child would sometimes be only inferable."

Chapter 12 : *From Prehistoric Crete to Classical Greece*

TOWARDS the end of the Minoan Age Cretan culture began to spread generally over the Ægean, and extended to the mainland. Cretan vases are found as far north as Bœotia, and the many Cretan relics discovered in Mycenæan tombs were not all war-souvenirs ; some of them, belonging to times before the fall of Knossos, were the peaceful product of Cretan workmen who had been induced by the Lords of Mycenæ to emigrate.

The men from the North who finally overthrew what we call the Minoan civilization, became to some extent the repositories of Cretan tradition. They carried on a less splendid phase of Cretan civilization, a phase which was distinguished by the name " Mycenæan." They had come to Greece from lands still further north, whence they had themselves been driven to seek new homes. They came down in successive waves of invasion, the men who formed the first wave being known as the " Achæans," the " yellow-haired Achæans "

of Homer. It was they—so at least some
authorities hold—who sacked Knossos, and
who afterwards, during the thirteenth and
twelfth centuries B.C., wandering about in
search of adventure, became the terror of the
whole Ægean. An Egyptian inscription of
those times says : " The Isles were restless :
disturbed among themselves."

Egypt herself felt the effect of the disturb-
ances. From the " isles in the midst of the
Great Green Sea " there no longer came the
peaceful Minoans to pay friendly tribute to
the King of Egypt ; instead there came the
Achæans, on an unpeaceful mission. Two
raids were made—according to the students
of Egyptian records—one about 1230 B.C.,
another about 1200 B.C. (See H. R. Hall,
The Ancient History of the Near East, p. 70.
Methuen, 1913.) Mr. Hall gives the more
definite date of c. 1196 for the second invasion.
Not long after we find the Achæans, in Agamemnon's famous expedition, fighting against
the Trojans in Asia Minor. They took the
city at last in 1184 B.C., if we accept the date
which Greek tradition pointed to. It is their
deeds in the latter war that were sung by
Homer. Two generations after the Trojan
war, shortly before 1100 B.C., Greece was overrun by the Dorians, who formed the second

great wave of Northern invaders. After that
came the Dark Age, out of which about 800
B.C. emerged classical Greece.

Classical Greece was the fusion of the two
main elements of prehistoric times, the artistic
Mediterranean people on the one hand, and
the robust Northern invaders on the other.
Just as the fusion was probably consummated
in the Dark Age, so the first poet of classical
Greece, Homer, whether one person or the
embodiment of many, heralded their new life
in poems which seemed to take their subject from that Dark Age. What Homer wrote
was probably less legendary than historical.
Whether the traditions of the Minoan Age in
Crete were kept alive through the Dark Age
in Ionia, whither it is thought that they were
carried by Achæan refugees at the time of the
Dorian invasion, which extended to Crete, or
whether they remained dormant in Crete itself,
and in the Mycenæan centres of the mainland
of Greece, it is in either case certain that they
were well preserved, for their traces are plainly
to be seen throughout Greek civilization.
From the Greek writers they descended to the
poets of Rome, and so to the art and literature
of Europe.

INDEX

93

The Minoans

Index

DATE DUE

Demco, Inc. 38-293

3.3

Milton Keynes UK
Ingram Content Group UK Ltd.
UKHW022154180124
436299UK00004B/164